CRACKED NOT

BROKEN

CRACK NOT BROKEN

By

Joy Simmons

CRACKED NOT BROKEN

Printed in the United States of America

First Printing, 2016

ISBN: 978-0-578-17470-9

Email: www.joyvsimmons.com

Graphic by Jason Howard:
jvhoward82@gmail.com

DEDICATION

I would like to dedicate this book to my extremely brilliant and beautiful mother...

Mom, you are my strength, my light, my hope, and my motivation. You always believed in me and reinforced my GOD given strengths and talents, which gave me the courage to follow my dreams. You will always be my motivation to live life with purpose on purpose. I love you always.

CRACKED NOT BROKEN

Sometimes things happen to us that are beyond our control. It does not mean that GOD does not love us or that there is anything wrong with us. On the contrary, my personal opinion is that sometimes things happen because GOD not only loves us but He desires to use us as a vessel for His kingdom. Let me explain, there is no testimony without a test, God does not give us more than we can bear and when it gets too heavy, He will always provide a way out. Therefore, if you are reading this book, GOD is providing you a way to get out of your situation. It is time for your RESTORATION!!!

CRACKED NOT BROKEN

TABLE OF CONTENTS

INTRODUCTION

Upon deciding to write this book, I discussed the content with my best friend. He thought it was a bad idea to allow so many people into my personal life. He said, I should remember that people are people and they will judge me. Initially after he and I had this conversation, I rethought the idea of exposing all the hurt and pain I have suffered. Then I remembered, all the hurt, pain, and death Jesus suffered for the atonement of our sins and I thought to myself...who am I not to share? My misery is my ministry and our words have power.

Although, it is not my belief that our life is destined from birth, many say in the path of life (whether good or bad) our steps are paved before we are conceived in our mother's womb. I believe God is in everything and through Him all things are possible and he is more than capable to utilize our misery as our ministry. Every situation in life happens for self-growth, encouragement of others, and Kingdom edification. People have mistakenly convinced themselves that salvation and the love of the Lord equates to freedom from pain, agony, sorrow, and suffering; however, this is a lie from the pit of hell. Jesus suffered pain and He suffered to the point He was sweating blood in the Garden of Gethsemane -*Luke 22*. He was betrayed and abandon by those who should have loved and supported Him. He was spit on, beat, kicked, hung on a cross, and stabbed by those He loved, yet He did it all for us. As the world would say, 'He took it in the face without hesitation, fault, or blame.' This is something we could/would never do because at the first indication of trouble we instantly go into blaming others or blaming ourselves.

Paul said, "...for I have learned to be content whatever the circumstances" *NIV-Phil 4:11*. This is what we need to learn...be content whether we are going through or coming out, secure whether we are surrounded by others or alone, encouraging whether we are happy or sad, giving whether we are rich or poor, and loving whether we are full of joy or full of sorrow. This book is purposed to free your thoughts and behavior toward your unfortunate circumstances. It will promote healthy responses to situations that may be present in your life and empower you to make better decisions pertaining to your life experiences. Utilize this book and CD for the encouragement of knowing you are not

CRACKED NOT BROKEN

alone, you are loved, and your words have
power.

BETRAYAL

When I was a teenager, one of my best friends was a male. He and I were so close we called each other brother and sister and addressed both of our parents as mom and dad. At the time, he was closer to me than my biological brothers. A group of us used to hang out together. We would drink Pipers (champagne), smoke weed, go to the drive-in and/or chill somewhere and listen to music. Sometimes the group would stay overnight at someone's house or in a hotel. We would fall asleep fully dressed, no hanky-panky, no touching, feeling, or sexual statements, gestures, or innuendos. That was it, a true friendship with nothing more or nothing less. This guy was my cousin's (my other best-friend) ex-boyfriend. So, obviously I trusted him completely. One day after about 2-3 years of knowing him, he picked me up so we could hang-out as usual. He asked me if I wanted to go to the drive-in to see a movie, of course I said yes; after all he was like a brother, a best friend, I was good friends with his present girlfriend, he called my mom 'mom', he was at our house all the time, and I even drove one of his cars. Hell, he was my brother! On the way to the drive-in, we stopped and got 2 bottles of my favorite alcoholic beverage, Pipers. We begin watching the movie; I begin drinking (this wasn't the first time I went alone to the drive-in with him). He continued to urge me to drink and I did until I barely made it to the restroom, staggering like a drunk outside of a liquor store. At some point during the drive-in I recall him saying, "I can't take you home like this, mom will kill me. I'll get a room so you can sleep it off before I take you home." I don't remember driving to the hotel, going into the room, or taking my clothes off but I do remember awakening with him on top of me with his penis in my vagina and the awful feeling of betrayal from my closest friend date raping me. I barely fought him off before I passed out again. I don't remember how many times he penetrated me or what it felt like, I can't tell you if he raped me all night or left after to initial penetration and came back for me in the morning, I simply don't remember. But what I do remember is him asking me if we could do it again when I was awake. I begin to cry.

Have you ever been betrayed by someone you trusted?

_____

_____

_____

_____

_____

_____

If so, how did it make you feel and how did you handle it?

_____

_____

_____

_____

_____

_____

How should we handle betrayal?

_____

_____

_____

_____

_____

Why do you think I didn't stop being his friend?

_____

_____

_____

_____

_____

If so, did this affect your trust in people?

_____

_____

_____

_____

_____

What role did this play in the course of life?

_____

_____

_____

_____

_____

What do think you would have done different and why?

_____

_____

_____

_____

_____

UNLOVED

After years of physical, emotional, and mental abuse, after feeling dejected, unwanted, and isolated, after feeling worthless, hopeless, ugly, fat, and unloved, after suicidal thoughts and promiscuity, I found God. In my heart, I believe God has a purpose for me and my misery is my ministry. One day I set in my bed crying profusely, rocking back and forth, and questioning "what is wrong with me, why am I so unlovable," I was so lonely I didn't want to live, I barely had enough emotional and mental strength to get out of bed each morning. See prior to this I had been living for the Lord, walking in my calling and attending seminary. The lord had been using me as a vessel in areas of healing, prophesying, and discernment. But I decided God was taking too long to bless me with my husband so I had walked away from my spiritual call and went back to the world (sin) to find my husband...I was like a dog going back to his own vomit (Proverbs 26:11), how gross is that? Of course, the enemy was waiting for me with open arms, he probably rejoiced at my thought to return to what God had delivered me from. Now that I think about, I was truly worse off once I went back to sin than I ever was prior to accepting Christ as my Lord and Savior. The bible tells us, "When an impure spirit comes out of a person, it goes through arid places seeking rest and does not find it. Then it says, 'I will return to the house I left.' When it arrives, it finds the house swept clean and put in order. Then it goes and takes seven other spirits more wicked than itself, and they go in and live there. And the final condition of that person is worse than the first." Luke 11:24-26. That was me, I started off cracked but by the end I was shattered but not broken. Therefore, I attempted to repair myself by returning to church. One would think that would be the answer, however, through Christ we can do all things, not through ourselves no matter how good our intentions are. I went to church after church, looking, searching, and hoping for someone to show me the way. Each church I went too further damaged me, deeper and deeper. As I stated earlier, I was physically, emotionally, and mentally abused, now the enemy wanted to take me out completely, he wanted to add spiritual abuse to the list. There was a female pastor whom I trusted and respected. Prior to her moving out of town, she directed me to a church saying I would be safe because the pastor was a good friend of hers. She continued to explain he had been through a rough transition in the church and was in a rebuilding stage. Wow, that sounds like me, I thought. I went to the church, the word was amazing and the pastor was single and somewhat cute. I said to myself...finally, God has heard my prayers; I always knew I would be a pastor's wife, a first lady, you know, the woman of the church, someone that could love God's people with true love and teach the ladies to become women. (It is funny how the enemy work, I actual thought I could teach them how to be whole when I was still cracked). This pastor and I instantly became good friends, talking all the time, spending time together, going places such as restaurants and social events. One night when we were talking, he told me "I don't like surprises if I'm going to be in a relationship, I want to know everything up front," so I decided to transparently express me, I did this because I thought we were going to be in a relationship. I called him up and said I need to talk about my life so I can get my healing; I met him at the office in the church and told him EVERYTHING I could remember from age three and up. I cried on his shoulder, on his lap and in his arms for about 3 hours and he consoled me as a man of God would and should. About two to three weeks later our relationship went from a good friendship to being intimate, his soft touch, his lips, and the look of desire in his eyes. "Oh Lord, is this he or shall I look for another, I questioned myself." After several episodes over a few months of doing everything but penetration, he reminded me that he had a "special friend" and that special friend was not me, funny how he neglected to mention this before taking advantage of me at my weakest point.

Did he actually take advantage of me or did I take advantage of him?

_____

_____

_____

_____

_____

Have you ever felt deceived by someone you thought you could trust?

_____

_____

_____

_____

_____

Was this God's plan for my life or was this the reaping of my bad decisions?

_____

_____

_____

_____

_____

What do you think contributed to this type of behavior?

_____

_____

_____

_____

_____

If this was you, what could you have done differently?

_____

_____

_____

_____

_____

How do you resolve the effects of feeling unloved?

CRACKED NOT BROKEN

_____

_____

_____

_____

VIOLATED

Although I was about 10 years old, I can remember it as if it was yesterday. I was asleep in my cousin's room, sharing a bed as 10 year olds do. Her older sister came into the room, awakened me, and began to fondle me. I can recall her touching me in the places my mother told me not to let anyone touch. I didn't scream, I didn't fight, I didn't cry, and I didn't even try to stop her. She made me do things no child should do. I often wonder why I didn't stop her or yell out for help but I realized, though I was a child, it still felt good to my flesh. See our senses are developed at birth and the unfortunate the power of touch works on everyone, girl, boy, man, woman, child, or adult. To my knowledge, this only happened once and I actually repressed this incident in a little box and stored it deep-deep in my brain. However, as I got older, somehow that box must have lost its durability because things started leaking out. I became insecure about my sexuality; I thought it was my fault that she did those things to me. I consistently blamed myself and thought, "I must be a lesbian" I believed I could fix those thoughts by always having a male in my life. By the time, I realized that it wasn't my fault and that I'm not a lesbian, so much time had passed and so much damage had already occurred. This early unfortunate situation set the tone for a long life of abuse, low self-esteem, low self-confidence, poor self-image, and distrust. As an adult, I begin going to church to find out who I am in Christ, as I grow in my spiritual walk I realized I needed to confront the offender and forgive her so I can forgive myself and hopefully begin my 12 step program for emotional healing. This was a very difficult process. I did not want to argue and/or fight, I just wanted to feel normal (whatever normal was). So I confronted her eye to eye and said, "I know what you did to me when I was a little girl and it was wrong, it was not my fault, and I forgive you. Although, I never said what she did and before I could say what she did and what I was forgiving her for, she begin to cry and deny doing anything. She followed behind me as I walked down the street, saying, "Vanita, I didn't do anything, I swear I didn't do anything" I know that was her guilt. Praise GOD, I have forgiven her, it took time but I did it for myself.

Have there been times in your life when something beyond your control affected your life?

_____

_____

_____

_____

_____

If so, how did you cope with it?

_____

_____

_____

_____

_____

Did you actually cope or did you lock it in the little box in your brain, awaiting leakage?

_____

_____

_____

_____

_____

What is your healing process?

_____

_____

_____

_____

_____

How did you confront the offender?

_____

_____

_____

_____

_____

Have you forgiven the offender? If not, will you?

_____

_____

_____

_____

_____

More important, have you forgiven yourself?

_____

_____

_____

_____

_____

LOW SELF-CONFIDENCE

Your first sexual experience is supposed to be your best and I do mean your very best, it is the one thing that sets the stage for your sexual being. When I think about my first-first time (you will see what I mean in another talking point), I ask myself, "what was wrong with me," and if I could change anything from my past this would be in the top two. I was 13 years old, vulnerable and stupid. I was obvious cracked and in desperate need to be loved. My cousin fixed me up with her boyfriend's cousin who lived down the street from me. She had been telling me that I should have sex and it was so wonderful, that I shouldn't be afraid, I should just do it and she had the perfect person. As goofy as it was, I agreed. We walked down the street where I met this guy for the first time. I thought he was cute and convinced myself that I should give into this peer-pressure and have sex to see what's so good about it. I asked him, "will it hurt?" of course he said no. I asked him, "will he think I am a slut?" he said no. "I asked him did he like me," and he said I could be his girlfriend, so I said, ok and I took my clothes off. I was scared and doubtful, everything in me said, I should not do it but it was the "in" thing to do. I wanted him to stop but I didn't stop him, I know it wasn't the right thing to do but I did it. Once he took my virginity (or once I gave up my virginity), he got up out of the bed, gave me a kiss and went down stairs. He didn't even wait for me to get dressed. As I walked down the stairs and out the house, I could hear his younger cousins calling me a slut; I was devastated. As I walked home, his little cousins followed me repeatedly shouting, Joy is slut; such shame I felt. He never called me, he never came to see me, and he never even thanked me for giving my virginity to such a loser. However, when we were adults he approached me and asked if he could take me out. WOW, this jerk has a lot of nerves, I thought!!! I told him I would pray for him and pray that his daughter never experience the hurt and shame, I experienced from him.

Have you ever been pressured into doing something you knew was wrong?

_____

_____

_____

_____

_____

If so, why did you do it?

_____

_____

_____

_____

_____

What will you do different?

_____

_____

_____

_____

_____

Have you ever trusted someone that misled you?

_____

_____

_____

_____

CRACKED NOT BROKEN

Have you ever given up something so valuable and can never get back?

_____

_____

_____

_____

_____

If so, how did that make you feel?

_____

_____

_____

_____

_____

DECEIVED

I was about 15 years old and doing things most young teenagers do, which means smoking weed and drinking. My cousin (yes, the same cousin I let convince me to give up my virginity to a total stranger) introduced me to marijuana (weed). By this time, my self-esteem, self-worth, and self-confidence were very low. I had been smoking weed and drinking for probably 1 year and I was a pro (so I thought); I had weed rollers, weed pipes, unlimited supply of 'tops' (weed papers). Now that I think about it, I don't know how I was able to pay for it because I didn't have a job but I always had weed. It was a cold snowy winter night, my cousin asked me to go over her boyfriend's cousin house with her. She said he had some weed and Golden Champagne and only stayed a few blocks from my mom, although it was a cold and snowy night, we walked over to his house. He and my cousin went to roll some weed (a joint) and I poured the Golden Champagne while I sat at the table waiting for them to finish. They came back in the room and handed me the weed, I lit it and began to smoke and drink, then my cousin put the heater on the table close to my face. That was nice; I thought to myself, after all, it is somewhat cold in this basement. It seemed like seconds later as I was laughing; everything went black for a fraction of a second. I remember feeling anxious and weird. I got up from the table and walked outside; I was burning hot so I took my coat off. I recall a car driving by with men in it; they asked me if I wanted a ride. I said yeah, and then begin chasing after the car trying to jump on the trunk. I could hear my cousin screaming STOP Joy, so I stopped. As crazy as it sounds, I had a pocket bible in my coat. I recall pulling out my bible and reading it as my cousin and I walked down the street heading home. We passed by a Catholic Church name Precious Blood that was around the corner from my house. This church had a statue of Mary in the yard, I walked near the statue, lay in the snow and begin to make snow angels while uttering words I can't recall except "GOD if you get me through this I will never smoke weed again." My cousin then took me to her boyfriend's house, which was in the same neighborhood. We rang the doorbell and when his mother came to the door, I can very vividly recall begging her for help and then calling her every name but the child of GOD. Then I thought I needed to throw up, so I put my finger down my throat to make myself vomit but after vomiting, I was still high. Somehow we made it back to my house, my mom had gone out with her friends and all I could think is, "if I just drink milk I will feel better (don't ask why milk, I have no idea). I took the gallon of milk out of the refrigerator, sat in the middle of the floor and begin to drink it straight from the neck. I remember calling my friend (who is now deceased) but I can't remember the conversation or anything else pertaining to that night. However, I do remember feeling as if I was having mini-blackouts for several years after. It is so amazing how I can remember things that happen years ago but forget what I had for dinner yesterday; it must be all the damn weed I smoked as a teenager.

Have you ever promised GOD something in exchange of something else?

_____

_____

_____

_____
_____

If so, did you keep your part of the deal?

_____
_____
_____
_____
_____

Have you ever revisited a situation and
were able to see GOD's grace on your life?

_____
_____
_____
_____
_____

What would you have said to your relative?

Would you forgive someone who
(un)intentionally caused harm that may
affect you for the rest of your life?

If any, what steps of forgiveness would you
take toward this person?

_____

_____

What will you do differently?

_____

_____

_____

_____

_____

ABUSED

Finally, I met someone that cared, so I thought. I was about 16 years old when a classmate introduced me to his friend's cousin. I remember him talking about how wonderful this guy was. He said he was kind of tall, had green eyes, light complexion, nice hair, lived in the suburbs, his father owned his own company, and he was a semi-pro boxer that would soon go professional. Of course, I wanted to meet this person; after all, I deserved a good man in my life. He introduced us and everything he said about him was true. It was a match made in heaven, at least for the first 10-12 months. Then he moved in with his cousin who stayed in Detroit and enrolled in the same high school as me. Awesome, I thought but he became abusive and promiscuous. He dated (slept with) at least half of the girls in the school. One day while I was at school he asked me to come over to his cousin's house (which was a couple of blocks from the school) so I skipped class and went to see him. When I got there, he wanted to have sex but I didn't, so he took a shoe and hit me on the leg. He hit me so hard that my leg instantly bruised. I cried, he kissed me, apologized and we made-up with sex of course. But that wasn't the only incident, another day we were walking down the street leaving my mother's house on our way to his cousin's house, I forget what made him mad this time (I probably did something, I thought) but he beat me like I was a man. I fell to the ground and he continue to beat me (remember, he was a semi-pro boxer), he beat me until a man driving by stopped, got out of his car and stopped him. He ran off and then as crazy as was, I ran after him, apologizing as if I had done something wrong. As I had caused this man that supposed to love me, to beat me like I was a stranger, like someone he hated and wanted to cause harm. If that was not enough, he continued to beat me, whenever he felt like it beating me and for whatever reason he felt like beating me. The worst part is that I stayed, I didn't know any better. I had convinced myself that it was my fault and I needed to change because I must be doing something wrong that causes him to beat on me. 'Plus, he always apologized whenever he hit me so he must really love me. He will stop one day, when I stop making him mad.' At least that was my thought but it never stopped, until I left.

Have you ever experienced pain by someone that should love?

_____

_____

_____

_____

_____

Do you blame yourself for someone actions or abusive behavior toward you?

_____

_____

_____

_____

_____

If so, why do you blame yourself?

_____

_____

_____

_____

_____

Why does someone allow others to treat them bad and then make excuses for them?

_____
_____
_____
_____
_____

What can/will you do different?

_____
_____
_____
_____
_____

UNWORTHY

It was my first day in a management
position at an inner city hospital; I walked in
the front door toward the elevator behind
the most adorable man I had ever seen in
my life. I thought to myself, I want to marry
this man and have his children. When he
got on the elevator, I said to myself, "this is
my chance to make my move." See, I had
learned to be somewhat aggressive because
passive people are walked over and/or used
as doormats. (At the time, I had just started
my own non-profit organization and had a
local television show and yes, I used that as
a pick up line with him). I asked him if he
was interested in mentoring the youth. I
gave him a card and hoped he would call
me but he didn't call me and I wasn't
aggressive enough to call him. My initial
thought was, I'm not pretty enough, smart

enough or small enough, then I remembered God had restored me. I had been living for the Lord and practicing abstinence for nearly 2 years. I gave up looking for him call, I figured God has someone else for me. Then I got a call from the laundry department at the hospital. The caller said, "a physician lost his wallet, your card was the only number in it and I need you to contact him to inform him that his wallet was found in the on-call room." Just the excuse I needed. I called him, he answered and I relayed the message but he still blew me off for at least another month or two. Then one day he was rounding on the unit that I managed, he approached me and inquired about mentoring (as soon as I got to my office, I started praising GOD and dancing like David). He was the best *man* that ever happened to me. I adored him from the very moment I saw him walking down the corridor in the hospital. As I got to know him, I adored him more. Not only was he the cutest man I've ever met but he was supportive in all I dreamed of doing; even my walk with Christ. He would come to my office almost every day and we would just sit and talk for hours. One day he told me, "Joy, you want to go to the moon but I don't. I'll help you get there and I'll be here when you get back" (so refreshing). I would try to kiss him but he would push me away and tell me to go pray and I did and he was everything I prayed for. I was determined to make him want me. About 7 months later, I wouldn't let him leave out of my office without a kiss, so I kept trying to kiss him and he would turn his head but I caught him on the lips and he kissed me back. Remember, I had been abstinent (not even a kiss) by this time it was over 2 years. At that point, I saw stars, fireworks, lightning bolts, and heaven open up ready to receive me. I had never experienced such a surge of emotions. Shortly after that we had sex (yes, I broke my abstinence), it was like a second first time. He was everything my first-first time was not; he was gentle, loving, affectionate, and caring. Our relationship progressed for about a year then he told me he loved me so I picked a fight and broke off the relationship (deep down I still had residual from my past that had not been uprooted). About 3 weeks later, I attempted to make him jealous and lied to him about getting involved in another relationship. Even today, years later he has never forgave me. I never thought I was worthy of love, after being beat down for so long, I was unable to accept someone loving me.

Have you ever felt unworthy of love?

_____

_____

_____

_____

_____

Has fear ever made you do something you regret?

_____

_____

_____

_____

_____

Has God ever given you another chance and you made the same mistakes?

_____

_____

_____

_____

_____

Have you ever taken someone for granted?
If so, what did it cost you?

_____

_____

_____

_____

_____

What would you do differently?

_____

_____

_____

_____

_____

DISCOURAGEMENT

As I lay in the bed thinking of my life decisions, I remembered I had not spoken with my mom yet this particular morning; she and I talked everyday starting first thing in the morning about 8:30am and at that time, it was about 9:30am. I turned over, grabbed the phone and called her. My cousin answered the phone and I could hear my mother screaming in the background. I jump up and begin to yell "WHAT'S WRONG, WHAT'S WRONG with my mother? Why is she screaming? My cousin said the police are here, its Willie, he is dead. I fell to the floor and began to pray, that's all I knew how to do when I was in trouble, and believe me, I was in trouble; terrible emotional trouble. Willie was my best friend, my protector, and my brother. No matter what, I could depend on him for any and everything. He would always tell me "Baby Sis, I will kill a brick for you" and he meant it. I can remember when I was about 7 or 8 years old, I was sitting on the arm of the sofa crying. Willie came home, took one look at me, went right into the back room, and begin whipping on my other brother and sister. When he finished kicking their butt, he came to me and said, "What did they do to you?" I said, (in a crying voice) nothing, I can't find my baby doll. That was Willie, kick butt first then take names later. About 2 weeks prior to his death, he and I were at mom's house standing outside talking. He was crying and said he was tired of fighting. (Willie had been in and out of jail most of his life. He was the sweetest person anyone could meet but often made bad decisions while living life in the fast line). I prayed with him, I told him if he went to truck driving school (as he desired) I would help him and he could live with me. He said okay and I'm sure he meant it but I imagine it's hard to slow down when you've been in the fast lane for so long (things can go from 0-60 in seconds but what actually goes from 60-0 in seconds without major injuries). So, the police were at my mom's house and Willie was dead, shot about 5 times, and found by the policy at the scene of the shooting. To add salt to the wound; we know the person who murdered him. I kind of blamed myself; see about a year prior, God had told me that my walk wasn't just for me but for my family as well and if I couldn't do it for myself I need to do it for them. He (God) asked me if I was willing to let my family die. Then, about 2 weeks prior to Willie's death, my son had a dream that God told him our loved ones were going to die unless I was obedient to His word. After Willie was deceased I met a Pastor, I told her what happened including the words and dream from God. She said "who do you think you are, Jesus? God doesn't put that much effort into nobody, people are accountable for their own sins." I went home prayed and God led me to read the book of Jonah, in this bible book everyone around Jonah was going to perish because of Johan's decision. However, I accepted her truth and continued to live in sin.

Do you ever feel like God is punishing you?

_____

_____

_____

_____

_____

Has God ever told you to do something but you refused? If so, what happened?

_____

_____

_____

_____

_____

If so, what would you have done
differently?

_____

_____

_____

_____

_____

Do you believe your walk with God is
connected to others around you?

_____

_____

_____

_____

_____

Has the enemy ever tricked you into doubting yourself or your relationship with God?

_____
_____
_____
_____
_____

If so, how and what did you do to get back in line with God?

_____
_____
_____
_____
_____

Have you ever blamed yourself for something beyond your control?

CRACKED NOT BROKEN

_____

_____

_____

_____

_____

MISLED

At the time of my best friend, protector, and brother's (all one person) death, I was engaged to a very controlling and abusive man. I knew he was controlling but I didn't know how controlling until the worst day of my life happened. After hearing the news of my brother's death and getting off the floor from praying, I rushed to my mom's house. She was an emotional wreck even more so than I was, so of course I decided to stay the night with my mom. On my way to my mom's house, I called my fiancée to tell him the unfortunate news pertaining to the death of my brother. My fiancée had a good relationship with my brother because he frequently (at least 4 times a week) came over to our house to chill or beat my fiancée in chess. Once my fiancée got off work he came to my mom's house, it was later in the day and many people were there. When he walked in, I was sitting on the sofa, he mumbled, "hi Joy as he walked passed me into the living room where my mom was sitting. I didn't trip because I knew at the time she needed more comforting than I. He stayed for a few hours, never talking to me while he was there. Then he came in the living room with me and my girlfriends and said, "I'm leaving, are you coming?" When I told him no and that I was staying the night, he said whatever and walked out the door. Naturally, because of my own insecurities, I followed him out. I asked him why was he being so mean to me and not talking to me. He blew me off and said "just stay, don't come home." I said a few choice words and went back into my mom's house. He didn't call me the rest of the night and didn't answer my calls. That morning I was an emotional, spiritual, and mental wreck, I could not stop crying, I felt like I was having a nervous breakdown, as if my body and soul were separating. I was in desperate need of God's love and peace so I called my cousin's husband, Pastor J. Williams and all I can say is thank God for his anointing, through him God he saved my soul. That day I went home to get some clothes, while there I got into an argument with my fiancée, I cried out and said "I hate you right now, how can you do this to me when you know what I'm going through? "All he heard is me say is 'I hate him,' "you hate me; you hate me than give me my ring back "he said. I told him that I will give it back when I move, and then he said" move right now, you and your kids get out." I was so devastated, I could not say a word, I took the ring off and put it in his hand then he said that he was sorry and was just calling my bluff. I was even more devastated; I had never felt such deep internal pain.

Have you ever felt like if you didn't get help at that very moment you would do something you regret? If so, how did you handle it and what would you do different?

_____

_____

_____

_____

_____

Have you ever had hate in your heart toward someone you thought you should love?

_____

_____

_____

_____

_____

If so, why and what did you do?

_____

_____

_____

_____

_____

Have you ever felt like someone was trying
to kill you emotionally?

_____

_____

_____

_____

_____

If so, did you stay or did you leave?

_____

_____

_____

CRACKED NOT BROKEN

FAILURE

I had excellent health, a new Mercedes R350, a big house, a good job, my own non-profit organization, a local television show, an awesome supportive man, and enough money in the bank to shop and go on trips whenever I felt like it, I didn't even have to manage/balance my check book. I felt like I was on top of the world, like "the world was mine's" all to wake up one morning and it was all gone, I mean completely gone. One morning I waken in what seemed like hell. I believe it was because I walked away from the church and returned to a life of less than what God had for me (a life of sin). Then something happened, my season changed. In this particular season of life, I was told I had a blockage in my brain and they though I may have had bilateral breast cancer, and I was now in a mentally and emotionally abusive taxing relationship which led me to lose my job causing a downward spiral. My house foreclosed, I had to give my Benz back and my credit was now in the toilet. I also had to let go of my non-profit organization and television show, and spent all my savings on necessities because I could find a job. I never seen that coming, I always thought, 'I'm a nurse with an MBA, I can always get a job" but that could not have been further from the truth. I had too much experience and education for a staff nurse position and I had been unemployed too long from another management position, so no one would hire me. At least no one would hire me until I practically begged an old friend (who was a manager for a local hospital emergency department) for a job. After begging for a few months and I literally mean begging, she gave me a contingent position. This was

great because I was working and received a
bi-weekly check. However, my schedule
varied from one end to the other. One
check I may bring home $2000 and the next
check I may bring home $300. I did not
understand what I had done so badly for my
life to be in such disarray but God works in
mysterious ways. My sister, who had
previously been on drugs and tortured me
most of my childhood, teenage, and young
adult years one day came to me and said, "I
will pay for your food this month and give
you $100 on my bridge card until you start
working again." Maybe not at that moment
but soon after I realized God was humbling
me. I believe I had gotten so full of myself
God needed to show me who was really in
charge or He was simply preparing me for a
time such as this. The very person I thought
hated me, God brought to help me and no
matter how prideful I was, I needed to feed

my children. This was probably one of God's most difficult lessons for me to learn. When God shuts doors, NO man can open them, no matter how hard you push or pull, that door is staying shut until God opens it.

Have you ever taken something/someone for granted?

_____

_____

_____

_____

_____

Have you ever felt like the rug was snatched from under your feet?

_____

_____

_____

_____

_____

CRACKED NOT BROKEN

Have you ever suffered a loss? If so, how did you handle it?

_____

_____

_____

_____

_____

Have you ever walked away from someone, something, or somewhere when you should have stayed?

_____

_____

_____

_____

_____

Have you ever been humbled? If so, how did you handle it?

_____

_____

_____

_____

_____

Is there anything you would have done differently?

_____

_____

_____

_____

_____

LOW SELF-ESTEEM

I grow up believing I was unlovable, ugly, fat, and stupid at least that's what I was told by many of my relatives, not just verbally but nonverbally as well. I had suffered so much abuse I believed what they said about me. I was overweight; lighter than everyone in my family (except my bi-racial siblings) I was a high school dropout, and pregnant teenager. Even my best friend's (at the time) mother said I would amount to nothing. There were many straws on this camel's back but the one that probably broke it was when my abusive boyfriend and I were in the basement of my mom's house, he decided to beat me up, I can't remember what I did that time or what I didn't do. However, I remember vividly calling for my brother to help me. I heard him talking upstairs in mom's dining room, so when my boyfriend slapped me in the face, I started yelling my brother's name. He said, 'what' and I said help me my boyfriend is trying to beat me up. He said oh, but he never came to help; he just let him beat me up. I was devastated. I had to learn to fight back at that very moment and I did, long enough to get away. So if my own brother did not love me enough to protect me, my family, my best friend and her mom frequently had negative things to say about me, and my boyfriend beat me up several times a week. How can I expect anyone to love me? At this point I felt I was unlovable and that I deserved everything I was getting. Since I felt everything was my fault I never told my mom that my boyfriend was beating me and no one protects me when she is at work. I was ashamed and grew to hate myself, I felt worthless, small and unworthy. My life experiences had pushed me into a dark emotional place. I became a needy, insecure, low self-esteem, and promiscuous individual. I would convince myself that if I had sex with him (whoever he was at the time) he would stay and love me. He stayed all right, he stayed all night, for all the free sex he could handle but when he got tired, he left without ever loving me and probably not even liking or respecting me. As I think about this, there was no way anyone could have loved me because I didn't love myself and my self-reflection didn't allow the average man to see anything other than what was on the surface which was a victim mentality.

What do you see when you look in the mirror?

_____

_____

_____

_____

_____

How do you fall in love with yourself?

_____

_____

_____

_____

_____

Have you ever allowed other people's behavior change how you feel about yourself?

_____

_____

_____

_____

_____

If so, how can you change your self-perception?

_____

_____

_____

_____

_____

Have you ever been neglected by someone who should have protected you?

_____

_____

_____

_____

_____

INSECURE

When everything in my life was falling down, falling apart, or simply broken, in the mist of this storm, I met a man, a strong handsome man. I looked at him and thought, "is this he or shall I wait for another." I know God is a God of multiple chances and I've been praying for a man to come into my life and love me. This must be him, I thought. This is the man I've been looking for; my savior, my protector, my lover, my soul mate, the one God has sent to me as a replacement for everything I had lost. I would ask him time after time, "will you protect" then one day he asked me, "protect you from what or from whom? Is someone looking for you? Is there something you need to tell me?" I told him I had been through so many bad things in life I just wanted someone to love me and protect me from being hurt even by him. He laughed and said, you are silly but he never answered. As time went by, I begin to notice certain familiar traits. Such as, one day we were talking and I said something like, I will love you forever. His response was, shut the f*** up nothing last forever. I blew it off like the broken woman I had become. Then his verbal abuse got worse but strangely, his financial support got better. I rationalized within myself and once again, I blamed myself for all the emotional and verbal abuse I was suffering through, just as a battered woman would do. I would always threaten to leave but would never go then I found myself trying to convince him to stay when he acted as if he was going to leave me. We had very good moments where I felt like a princess but his bad moments were emotionally bad. He never physically abused me; however,

bones are easier to heal than emotions.
Even with all of this, we had an exclusive
relationship. I had keys to his house and he
came over my house as often as he felt like
coming, which seemed like daily if I wasn't
at his house. One day he picked an
argument, asked for his keys back, and told
me he was going to date other people but
would tell me when he met someone else.
Shortly after, that day came but he didn't
tell me, I found out the hard way. At the
time I worked midnights, I was off the day
before so he had stayed the night with me
and left for his job that morning and I went
to work that night. While at work, I had a
weird feeling in the pit of my stomach
causing me to feel nauseous. Somehow, I
knew he was with someone else. Long story
short, he got out of the bed with me Friday
morning and was in the bed with someone
else Friday night...just nasty. When I

questioned him, he said many hurtful things but the one thing that really stood out was when he said, "damn, I don't know why you are tripping, you forced yourself on me anyway."

Have you ever inadvertently forced your needs or thoughts onto someone?

_____

_____

_____

_____

_____

Have you ever allowed yourself to be vulnerable or stayed in a situation when you know it's unhealthy?

_____

_____

_____

_____

_____

_____

Do you suffer from bondage of your past? If so, how is it affecting your life?

_____

_____

_____

_____

_____

Have you ever put someone on the same level as GOD? If so what happen?

_____

_____

_____

_____

_____

UNDESIRED

All I wanted was for someone to love me intimately; I prayed every night that God would bless me with my husband. After all, I was obedient to the spirit, practicing abstinence, attending church at least twice a week, and the lead intercessor (and I mean my prayers were getting through). I was also blessed with the gift of healing and prophesy and I had been the armor bearer of the *First Lady* (this topic is discussed more in the next book). I was on fire for the Lord; water baptized and Holy Ghost filled. However, I felt like something was missing, I looked around and saw what seemed like happiness of others. People appearing less anointed than myself were seemingly being blessed with the desires of their heart. At the time, I had a good friend that had invited me to this particular church. I had observed her life, I thought to myself, she smoke weed, drink, party, have sex, and seems to prosper (I only know these things because she told me). I questioned God about my observation. I asked Him why I have to walk in my calling and not sin while it seemed like the people that were living contrary to Your word are were being blessed. Do not get me wrong, she still went to church, she was in the choir, and she was an intercessor. She was the coolest person I knew and at that time, I had known her for at least 25 years. All the guys wanted to get to know her and all the girls wanted to be like her. I'm not sure if I wanted to be like her but I surely wanted to live the life of the most hood-famous as she did. I also wanted to have sex, drink, and party without the repercussions of the spirit. One day she and I were talking about the word of God and I asked her, why is it that you can live in sin and still be blessed but when I think about stepping out my life falls apart? Of course, she did not have an answer, which made me even more frustrated with my life. I was tired of being righteous, lonely, and bored. I wanted what she had or so I thought...

Have you ever been jealous of someone?

_____

_____

_____

_____

_____

If so, why were you jealous and what did you do?

_____

_____

_____

_____

_____

How did you handle those emotions?

_____

_____

_____

_____

_____

Did you walk away from you beliefs and succumb to the pleasures of someone else's life?

_____

_____

_____

_____

_____

If so, how did that make you feel?

_____

_____

_____

_____

_____

DISAPPOINTED

In 2005, I decided to date one of my brother's best friends. I thought I would be emotionally safe with him; after all, he was not just my brother's best friend and a friend of the family. He had been around for more than half my life. I was devoted to the Lord, I had just officially become divorced and just bought a house. I felt strong, secure, and beautiful (so I thought). My new house needed painting so my brother recommended his friend (yes, his best friend). I thought it was a good idea because I could receive a family discount while getting my house painted the way I wanted. It took him about three weeks to paint and I know it doesn't seem like a lot of time, however, somehow during that time he and I made a connection. He told me that he had liked me for many years and wanted to date me. My first thought was, 'he is not exactly my type but what do I have to lose, I hated being alone plus he is my brother's best friend so I should be safe.' I decided to date him and things went very well, we talked about a long term relationship, possible marriage but there is was one problem. I was working on my relationship with the Lord and he wasn't, so we fixed that and decided to recommit our relationship to the Lord as individuals and a couple. We went to his mother's church (where she was a minister) and received our rebirthing into the spirit of God. The first time we went, they put us in a room together, neither of us received the gift of the Holy Spirit so they decided to separate us, a few days later he received the Holy Spirit and 3 days after I received the Holy Spirit. That was in perfect order, right? The man is the head thus; God will give it to the man first. I thought I was on my way, finally dating a saved man that will know how to love me as Christ loved the church. We planned ways on how we as a team would edify God's Kingdom, the bible tells us that two is better than one, so we went to church and bible study as a couple. I was thinking I would be the perfect Pastor's wife, I would love on God's people and treat and love them the way I always wanted to be treated and loved. I would have a minister for a mother-in-law (someone to teach and guide me) but unexpectedly his mother began to act differently toward me. She begin to punish me because I was educated, he said she felt that I thought I was better than people and God doesn't care about my education, she eventually stop speaking or even acknowledging me. I didn't get it, I never use my education to belittle people, I never even thought I was smart, just determined to provide a better future for my children, my mother, and myself in that exact order. One day shortly after his mother stop speaking to me, he called me and said, "my mom thinks you feel like you are better than us." He continued with...our salvation is individualized and I think I'm going to be like Paul who said it is better not to marry and so I can focus on the Lord" I was devastated, I had been dropped yet again!

Have you ever asked yourself "what's wrong with me? Why am I so unlovable?

_____

_____

_____

_____

_____

How would you have respond?

_____

_____

_____

_____

_____

If anything, what would you have done
differently?

_____

_____

_____

_____

_____

Would you internalize this situation? If not,
how would you prevent internalize it?

_____

_____

_____

_____

_____

HOPE

I was a manager of a nursing unit at a local hospital and frequently participated in a local Medical Organization along with a couple of co-workers. This organization has monthly local meetings and annual national meetings. This particular year the organization was planning the national conference in Hawaii. I did not intend to go until one on my co-workers convinced me to go to, after some strong-arming. Once there we decided to attend one of the events, which included a meet and greet after party, where I met a man I never intended to see again. However, I realized communicating with him could produce excellent networking opportunities. After all, I was a talk-show host with my own non-profit organization and he was a Major in the Army. He and I exchanged phone numbers. For years, we stayed in touch via social media and occasional phone calls, which resulted in the development of a friendship. We had the opportunity to see each other 2-3 times over several years. During those years we talked about everything, he was the one man that I trusted enough to tell about every nook and cranny of my life. You name it, if it happened to me, if I wanted it to happen to me, or if I was afraid it would happen to me, he knew about. Several years after our meeting, his employer moved him to Metro Detroit, Michigan. (Wow, what a coincidence, the fact that we stayed in touch after meeting several years prior in Hawaii on a trip that neither of us intended on going and after being convinced to go and both agreeing at the last minute. What an amazing pull of God!). Once he was settled into his new environment in Metro

Detroit, he called to invite me out. (At first, I hesitated because at the time I had been in an off and on relationship for over 4 years but I decided that maybe the change would be healthy). He and I went to dinner and a movie, he was a perfect gentleman; I felt like I was the only person in the room. The way he smiled when he looked at me, the way he touched my hand, the way he pulled out the chair for me to sit down at the table, the way he opened the car door for me to get in and out, and his public display of affection was priceless. This was something I totally was not use to and it was so refreshing! A few months went by and I had not heard from him until a few days before my birthday he called me and inquired if I had birthday plans. I told him I had no plan, so he said "don't make any plans, I will call you in a couple days" I said "okay" and that was the end of our conversation. I was super excited to have a date with a man on my birthday; it had been a very long time since I spent my birthday with anyone other than my family. The day before my birthday I was beginning to get a little worried because I hadn't heard from him then on the morning of my birthday my phone rang and it was him with reservations at 7pm. Dinner was good, desert was great, and his company was amazing. That day, I felt like a Queen! What made the day extra special is that he knew everything about me and still accepted me for me, baggage and all. I recall one day while I was at his house, he said, "you know this could only be God, how else would we end up in the same state after all these years of meeting in Hawaii and staying in touch. You don't understand what had to take place for me to land in Detroit, there were so many behind the scene entities that had to take place for this to happen." Although we have had some challenging times and traveled some bumpy roads, I now know what it feels like to be treated like the queen again and I enjoyed every second of it.

Do you believe in coincidences?

_____
_____
_____
_____

_____
_____

Do you think everything is in God's divine purpose?

_____

_____

_____

_____

_____

Do you hope/except change or settle for status que?

_____

_____

_____

_____

_____

Have you ever trusted someone enough to be transparent?

_____

_____

_____

_____

_____

Do you feel celebrated or tolerated with the people around you? How does it feel?

_____

_____

_____

_____

_____

Do you feel you deserve to be treated like royalty?

_____

_____

_____

_____

_____

RESTORED

One summer day, my ex-boyfriend invited me to his house for a visit. I loved him with every fiber of my body. Although, he didn't love me the way I loved him, he was always there when I needed something, no matter what it was that I needed, what time I needed it, how much I needed, or why I needed it. He and I had some extremely rough times while dating but I knew 100% I could always depend on him. He was one of my best and closest friends. We talked often, went to dinner and/or a movie, I even stayed many nights with him without any type of sexually contact. We had concluded that his love for me was less than my love for him and he did not want to have a committed relationship therefore, we decided on being just friends. We would laugh, play, wrestle, joke, and enjoy each other's company. It was a true friendship as if he was with one of the girls, I trusted him with my life. I know about the women in his life and he knew about the man I had previously dated. So, this particular day I went to his house, he had grilled chicken in the backyard and was waiting for me to come eat (he would cook for me often because I truly enjoyed his cooking and he knew it). I arrived, he fixed my plate, I ate then we watched a movie on cable and talked as usual. I rested my head on his shoulder, he kissed me, and I kissed him back. That was the first mistake; the second mistake was that I enjoyed the kiss, which led to more pain and suffering. Again, he kissed me and I kissed him back then he took my hand and attempted to pull me to his bedroom. I tried resisting but my emotional attachment to him was much stronger than my physical and logical strength. I pleaded with him to stop and even explained that I was emotionally unstable to have sex with him because I was so in love him, sex would only complicate things, his response was "it sucks to be you." He continued to penetrate and I continue to plead with him not to place me in a compromising emotional, mental and physical position. However, he continued and I did not physically fight him off. I desired his touch so much that I allowed him to violate me while I laid there and cried. Afterward, he held me and said thanks for the hook up then he fell asleep. I told him it was not a hook up and that was a horrible thing to say after what just happen. I laid there for a moment trying to pretend it never happened or it was okay that it happened but my heart was so troubled I just got up and left. I'm not sure if he even realized what he did to me or how it affected me, even worse, I'm not sure if he even cared. To add salt to the wound, I attempted to call him the next day in hopes of him saying something like "I'm sorry or I love you" but instead he blew me off, he did not talk to me, ignored my text messages then stop answering my calls. Not only did he violate me by taking something so precious from me, he then rejected me, which was worse than the violation. Wow, I feel like I can relate with Tamar's story in the bible (2 Sam 13). Of all the things I have been through, this testimony by far this was the worse...but God never gives us more than we can handle (1 Cor. 10:13) and He uses every situation (good or bad) for His purpose. Prior to this incident, I felt that I needed a man to complete me, which caused me to struggle in my walk with Christ. He used this unfortunate situation to detour my fleshly desires and dependency toward men to the point I did not want to hear, touch, smell, see, or taste (kiss) a man, which allowed me to focus on healing and restoration. It allowed me to be restored to my first true love...Christ.

Has God ever allowed you to be tested? If so, did you pass the first time?

_____

_____

_____

_____

_____

Has God ever used something/someone to draw you closer to Him? If so, how did you respond?

_____

_____

_____

_____

_____

Are you ready for double for your trouble?

_____

_____

_____

_____

_____

Are you ready to be RESTORED to
wholeness and completeness?

_____

_____

_____

_____

_____

LOVED

After a long time coming, finally I found love. It's like I awaken one morning and realized love is within me; I am love and I am in love with who God has made me to be. For so many years I thought I was unworthy, unloved, unattractive, undesired, unsuccessful, and so many other 'uns' but the truth is what we think about ourselves on the inside shows up on the outside. Once I recognized and openly acknowledged my positive attributes, I allowed others to see my worth. In doing so I opened the door to a new world; a world of love, happiness, and acceptance; a world that allowed me to be myself, the way God created me, whole and complete without all the negative lies I have believed about myself. This new sense of liberty allows me to be loved internally and externally. It allows me to truly love and not obsess or possess a man that truly loves me. Now, I can experience what it feels to love and be loved.

Will you allow God to heal you of your past hurt, guilt, shame, and pain?

_____

_____

_____

_____

_____

Lord your word say, if I confess my sins, You are faithful and just to forgive me of my sins and to cleanse me from all unrighteousness. Lord, I humbly ask You to completely restore my soul and spirit so that I may fully serve You. Please help me to overcome my past and heal me so that nothing hinders Your plan and purpose for my life.

CONCLUSION

When I look back over my life, I wonder how someone so kind hearted and loving has never felt love, my entire life all I wanted was to love and be loved. I have fought so hard through so many different forms of abuse, rape, manipulation, misuse, pain, and self-hatred just to feel some form of love and attention. Although the past is behind us, it plays a unique and crucial role in our present and future decisions. See, if we don't know our worth it's impossible for someone else to know our worth. In order for the enemy to defeat us, he must first strip us of our strength, self-worth and self-belief, thus rendering us weak, hopeless, and ineffective. At that point, our only thoughts are to survive, rendering us people-dependent and/or substance dependent; continuously seeking the approval of others to make us feel whole and complete. The saddest part is that we do not see that we were born (created) whole and complete. We just have to believe in God then ourselves because this is truly, where our strength comes from...GOD. Once we believe we are worthless, hopeless, and unloved we are free game to the enemy, we are prey to the predators.

A very important fact is that 'We teach people how to treat us,' whether good or bad, our response/re-action toward their behavior validates the acceptance of their treatment. The bible teaches us to treat others the way we want to be treated; unfortunately, sometimes we don't know how we want to be treated. We get so lost in hurt, shame, and pain we become victims thus looking for and accepting victimizers into our lives. We set ourselves up for pain and suffering day-after-day, relationship-after-relationship, hoping and praying that someone will rescue us from ourselves, from the little dark space in our brain that we so tightly fit into. Sometimes, I am not sure if people take advantage of us or if we freely give and they freely receive. We have to learn to make decisions that are conducive to our own well-being and we have to trust GOD enough to know that if things do not work out the way we want, it is because He has a greater plan for our life. Desperation only empowers more pain and suffering. We have to find that place within ourselves that allows us know and understand our self-worth and until we find that place in our self-perception we will continue to search for someone to fill a void that only GOD can fill. We have to learn to let go, no matter how difficult it may be, how heavy it may feel, how much it seems to take our breath away...God needs us to give our hurt, shame, guilt, and pain to him. He wants to give us beauty for our ashes, joy for our mourning, and praise for our heaviness (Isaiah 61:3). He loves us more than we can ever imagine, so much that He gave the life of His ONLY son...so that we may have *and* enjoy life, and have it in abundance (to the full, till it overflows) John 10:10 (AMP). Nowhere in that last sentence does it include desperation, settling, or any form of abusive. STOP being a doormat. Stop being the victim because we are not victims we are victors. We are victorious! We are strong blessed individuals that can conquer every obstacle with the strength of GOD. Therefore, allow GOD to resolve and heal you of your insecurities thus creating wholeness and completion within you. The bible states, we are made in the image of

God and God is love. Thus, we are made in the image of love. Ok, go look into a mirror at this very moment, what do you see? You see an image of you, right? Look deeper with your God given spiritual sight, the very spirit that created you in His image, now tell me what do you see. Ok, if you still don't get it let me explain, everything about each of us has been designed (created) by God and I mean everything. Your hair color, texture, and length, the hair follicles in your scalp, the dynamics of the brain, your eyes, your eye lashes, nose, the hair in your nose, mouth, tongue, the taste buds on your tongue, teeth, gums that hold your teeth, tonsils, uvula, sinuses, throat, larynx, lungs, the bronchioles in the lungs, the heart, the 4 chambers of the heart, your skin tone/color, your size/shape, do you get where I am going with this? God created each of us differently for His purpose, for a time such as this, so that we can take everything the devil has attempted to use against us and use it to edify God's Kingdom. The disciples asked Jesus..."can we be born a second time from our mother's womb...Jesus answered,...saying except a man be born of water and of the Spirit... John 3:4" We are born once from our mother's womb but there is a rebirthing when we receive the Lord as our Savior then we take on the DNA of our creator. With this new DNA comes power, power to overcome, power to survive, power to succeed, power to persevere, power to forgive, and most of all power to Love ourselves and ourselves (in that order).

As strange as it sounds, in many of my testimonies, I think being the friend of these people gave me some form of acceptance, although it was negative acceptance, I was accepted and I was so afraid of being rejected and alone that I'd rather sacrifice my worth than stand up for myself. This totally added to my distrust in people and those that should've loved me, it also contributed to lowering my self-worth, self-esteem, and self-confidence. I was so ashamed of me that I thought had I told someone they would ridicule and blame me for the actions of others toward me, so I convinced myself that most of my unfortunate situations was my fault, that it was something I caused to happened; thus deepening my path of self-destruction. If I could do it all over again, I would have at least made them responsible for their actions and betrayal. For so many years, I felt unworthy of love but I had to learn that love does not come from without (someone else) but from within (self). Again, God created us whole and complete...therefore, we do not need anyone or anything to complete us. We are worthy of love and respect, although at times we may not feel like it, we must always remember and remind ourselves that GOD created us this way (whole and completed in His image). It is extremely important to place ourselves around people that are positive, encouraging, motivating, and empowering. It is equally important to be around and attached to people that celebrate us and not *tolerate* us, this will give us strength and encourage us not to settle for less than we deserve.

"For my thoughts are not your thoughts, neither are your ways my ways," declares the Lord. "As the heavens are higher than the earth, so are my ways higher than your ways and my thoughts than your thoughts (Isaiah 55:8-9 NIV). We never know why

God allows us to experience certain things in life. I believe many of our troubles are directly related to our own decisions and others are beyond our control, such as the story of Mephibosheth in 2 Sam 4. This 5-year-old child was not born lame in his feet but after he was picked up by his caregiver (trying to protect him); in a hurry to escape danger he fell from her arms and became disabled. These ailments had nothing to do with his decisions, his rebelliousness, his attitudes, his possible sinful behavior, or his thought process, it had to do with nothing other than the fact that he was innocent and affected by someone else's behavior. It is obvious that the nurse (caregiver) did not drop him intentionally; she was trying to save him, to protect him from harm, in the process caused more harm. I refuse to believe everyone that hurt me, hurt me intentionally nor have all those who hurt you hurt you intentionally. I'm sure some started out with good intentions but in the hurry of things they tripped and we fell right out of their arms. When David the King approached Mephibosheth, Mephibosheth referred to himself as a dead dog. Mephibosheth was not only lame physically but he had become lame mentally and emotionally as well. It is time to stop allowing a fall to paralyze us, it is time to stop crying, get up, dust off, and move forward. IT IS TIME TO COME OUT OF SELF-PITY!!!

Can you image what things would be like if Joseph went into a self-pity mode? For those of you that don't know the story of Joseph, I truly encourage to read Genesis 37-50. Joseph was an innocent, ambitious, loyal, person who was betrayed by people that should have loved and protected him.

As innocent as Joseph was, he was placed in a cistern, sold into slavery, falsely accused of rape and thrown in prison. However, in all that he went through, God blessed him in every situation he encountered. What was meant for his harm, God blessed for his good! When God is for you who can be against you? God will always show Himself in your situation, He will never forsake us nor will He leave us, He is always in the mist of our storm keeping our feet placed on solid ground. He has ordered our steps and purposefully planned our life even before the foundation of this world. (Romans 8:29). As previously stated, God uses every situation for His Kingdom Edification..."for we are wonderfully and fearfully made" (Psalms 139:14). Many of my testimonies has also taught me that when God allows us to be tested; there is no pass or fail because we will take the same test over and over again until we pass then God will take that unfortunate situation and restore us back to Him. His words states, "Because you got a double dose of trouble and more than your share of contempt, your inheritance in the land will be doubled and your joy go on forever. (Isaiah 61:7 Message Bible). Close your eyes and imagine what double looks like...it looks bigger and better, twice the amount of everything the devil has stolen from you and I mean everything. Bigger and better self-worth, self-esteem, self-confidence, physical, mental, emotional, and financial health, relationships, love, etc. If you can see it, you can be it, and if you can believe it, you will receive. It is time for your RESTORATION.

POETRY

CRACKED NOT BROKEN

Will you love?

If I stroke your ego, will you love me?

If I iron your clothes, clean your house, mop
your floors, and wash your windows, will
you love me?

If I give all I have, all my money, let you live
in my house or drive my car, will you love
me?

If I live your fantasies, you always wanted a
threesome, no baby I do not want a
threesome I just want you to love me, if I do
it, will you love me?

If I awake you to head or let another sleep
with you in our bed, will you love me?

What if I have sex with you every day
whenever you want it, will you love me?

CRACKED NOT BROKEN

If I let you have me any way you like, will you love me?

What if I cook your food and run your bath water and wash you up, will you love me?

If I do not have an opinion, will you love me?

What if I submit to you and do whatever you tell me to do, will you love me?

If I surrender my self-worth, beliefs and self-confidence, will you love me?

What if I give you my mind, body, and soul, will you love me?

If I let you beat me or cheat on me, will you love me?

If I give you my self-esteem, will you love me?

CRACKED NOT BROKEN

If you can call me names and take my dreams, will you love me?

The fact is, if I have to go through all of these measures for you to love me the question is not will you love me but DO I LOVE MYSELF?

OOPS

Oops I did it again. Another love struck decision has landed me in the dumps of the alley "I've lost it all this time" you would think I would have had enough the last time or two but no, I keep going back for more. One would think as time goes by we learn from our experiences but I guess that is not always the case. What is it that they call people who keep doing the same thing and expecting different results? Crazy is what they are, straight delusional. That is how I feel sometimes like a crazy woman who can't get pass go! I look back at my childhood and wonder if it is something I did or something that was done to me. I cannot find the answer; all I find is confusion, hurt and pain. I ask myself am I that unlovable? Why is it so hard for someone to love me? Ok, maybe it is not that hard because people love me but not those whom I seem to love. I usually make excuses for others but I am fresh out of excuses.

Why am I so unlovable I asked my GOD, "I love you" He replies but yet I don't receive His love in lieu I search for those I know deep down inside can't love me probably because they don't even love themselves. Cracked, that is what we are! They say, hurt people hurt people. What about broken people, I guess we break people; belittle, begrudge, deject, breaking their self-esteem, self-confidence, self-belief at the same time breaking ourselves.

I use to ask, how did I get here, to this awful deep dark empty space located in the center of my core, the space I try so desperately to fill? However, I've realized that is the wrong question, the correct questions are; who am I? What makes me happy? Why is there a deep dark empty space in my core when GOD created me whole? What does whole mean? How can I get out of this vicious cycle of mental, emotional, and/or physical abuse?

To start on the road of wholeness we must ask ourselves the above questions. I have dedicated my whole life to serving others, so much that I forgot to serve myself yet I hunger for things that aren't available for serving but the crazy thing is I settle for what's left on the menu although I know it will not fulfill my hunger. I have put my needs, wants, and desire so for back on the burner that I forgot what they were. Desperately seeking for something only GOD can give

It is time for to face the music and learn to dance at my own tune. What does that mean, I say to myself? What would others think or say if I start to dance? I dance off beat one might say, I have no rhythm another might say, I am two left feet others may say. As I think about the opinion of others it comes to me...this is my life, I have lost myself in others, always trying to please others and forgetting me, being selfless when I should have been selfish. Today I you to take the pledge with me to start living for yourself and allowing the Lord to lead you in the way you should go.

Signature: _____

Date: _____

CRACKED NOT BROKEN

Dear God,

It's me again, I'm sorry for continuously having to talk to you about the same things. I understand your word says you don't get tire of me but I know when people keep asking me the same thing it gets on my nerves. I guess that's why you are God and I am me. So this time like last time, it's a man. I know better and I don't want to continue like this. I'm so tired of making the same mistakes. What must I do Lord?...

Lord, your word says, "Trust in me and I will direct your paths" I try to trust but I seemed to have lost my compass

Lord, your word says, "Seek and you will find, knock and it will be opened, ask and it will be given to you

CRACKED NOT BROKEN

Lord, I've been seeking, knocking, and asking but sometimes it seems as if you don't hear me or you are not listening

Show me Lord, please show me that you love still rest on me and forgive me Lord, so that I can be all that You ordained me to be

SHOULD I STAY

My path is so dark...I can't find my way
through the clutter to knock and I'm so
dazed from the gaze that I'm too weak to
speak

So many thoughts running through my head
while my spirit feels half-dead...should I stay
or should I go

Lord, tell me what to do because I truly
don't know

Your word says, "They that wait on the Lord
shall renew their strength; they will mount
up on wings like the eagles and soar...

Lord, please strengthen me so I can get off
this threshing floor

CRACKED NOT BROKEN

Tell me what I need to do to be closer to you. My eyes and ears are open, my heart is ready

Lord, if you give me another chance I will follow your words steady, steady and free. Steady to expose the you that is in me.

AFRAID

Father, why am I so afraid to succeed? I
don't understand because I know you have
given me everything I need

But I still feel oppressed by the stress which
seems to make me depressed

Why am I so afraid to love but so willing to
hate? What's really going on, is this truly my
fate?

To sit back and not even try as life pass me
bye while I bicker, complain, and cry

I decided to blame it on the man, you know
the man that had my ancestors enslaved
and shackled with fear and lack

Although their pain and suffering I hold
near to my heart, this is an excuse I use to
be held back

CRACKED NOT BROKEN

I admit I've use it frequently so I don't have to look at what I really lack (Faith, obedience, courage, boldness, and ambition)

Yesterday, I had convinced myself that I was afraid to succeed but today I know God is all I truly need.

ESCAPE

If life is a collection of memories, maybe I should have amnesia. If love is the greatest gift, maybe I need to open more presents. I have asked others "will you protect me" but I never knew what I want protection from when I asked. So I questioned myself...protect me from what Happiness, Joy, Peace, Love, and Contentment...? Wow, that's funny all the things I wanted were none of the things I was getting. It was like a BIG STRONG armed man (a guard dog, a watchman, a demon) stood in the way of my true desires but he didn't come uninvited or unannounced. See that's the crazy part, I have invited these negative interactions into my environment, my living space, my heart, and my soul. I asked them "will you protect me" as if I truly needed protection. The bible tells us ask and we shall receive and it teaches us to pray specific prayers because we may get just what we are asking for...I never asked or specified what I wanted protection from, so I got protection but from all the things I really wanted and desired. As I look back over my past and I say "If life is a collection of moments" I have had some messed up moments or my collection is totally off so maybe I need to get a new collection, maybe I need new moments, or maybe I simple need new...

CRACKED NOT BROKEN

I SEE

Now I see...all along I thought it was me

Me that was wrong, me not being strong

Too weak to thrive, too weak to want to
stay alive

Alive to the stressors of life, alive to even
think I am worthy to be a wife

Where is my strength the bible say I
possess, where is my wisdom to confess

Confession to the sin's I have commit, wow,
I've been delusional I must admit

God, sometimes it seems as if you have
forsaken me but the bible tells me that
couldn't be

You are with me always, even when the
cloud covers my days

CRACKED NOT BROKEN

God, give me another chance, this time I won't fail because living my life like this has to be similar to hell.

RIDE

Back and forth, up and down, in and out, around and around, will this ride ever stop?

I try to put my foot out to slow it down; I try grapping the pole as I go around

I'm beginning to feel sick, nauseated, and dizzy. I'm discombobulated, my heart is pounding, my knees and shaky, my legs are weak, I can no longer speak

Can someone please help me off this ride because I can no longer ride this tide?

Because I'm drowning from the pain so deep inside...

RUNNING

Wait, I can't catch up, slow down I'm tired

Hold on, I'm short of breath

You're leaving me and I'm scared to be alone

I feel so weak, I can barely speak

The pain is driving me insane

I've lost my direction and my compass

Where in hell am I, it so dark in this place

Am I the only one in this space

I heard voices so I thought I wasn't alone

But when I turned around and looked they were all gone

They said they would never leave but it was a ploy

CRACKED NOT BROKEN

These people played me, as if I was a toy

Right and left, in and out I guess it's my fault so there's no need to pout

My fault for trusting, giving, and loving

The bible say love is the greatest gift of all

But when I love, all I seem do is fall

MIRROR

Oh my, I think I lost something so valuable

I didn't know its value until I couldn't find it

I lost me...

I have looked high and low but it's not me I see

Can someone help me find me?

Am I there behind that tree

Or am I lost deep in the sea

Where in hell can I be?

I have looked in the drug house

I have looked in the liquor store

I have looked under his sheet

I have looked under his bed

CRACKED NOT BROKEN

Maybe, I'm standing on the window edge

Can someone help me find me?

I don't know how no one has seen me

Where in hell could I be?

Maybe I'm locked in a room so full of doom

Because I lost my way in the darkness of
this day

Can someone please help me find me?

Which way do I go? Where could I be?

As I walked passed the mirror I glanced and
thought 'could that beautiful lady be me'

LEAVE

Sometimes we allow certain people to stay in our life that we know should not be a part of our life...they are emotionally abusive to us in order to keep us in their safety net that was built by us. Instead of you reminding yourselves, how you feel about yourselves you simply allow another person in your life to do it.

We never question it...WE JUST DO IT!!!

The situation that you are in right now does not define where you are called to be...

-Najah Howard

SINGLE

Sometimes the best thing we can do is to be single to give ourselves a chance to feel the great love we give to others!

Hurt people, hurt people and sometimes we get so immune to the pain that we begin to hurt ourselves

It is not about the journey we go through, it is about how we choose to go through the journey and what we bring from the journey.

-Najah Howard

ADDENDUM

As I begin the final editing of this book for
printing preparation, I begin to feel
extremely nervous, doubtful, and afraid to
share my testimony. I know and believed
God had purposed me to share this
information for the up lifting of others but
as I read, I was reminded of all the horrible
things I had suffered then I became
ashamed. I was ashamed that it seemed as
if I had not learned from previous
experiences; ashamed that I did not hate
the individuals that harmed me; ashamed
that I forgave them but not myself, and I
was still hurting. I had not truly given myself
the opportunity to heal; I just covered up
the pain and emotional agony with things
such as church (not God) and education,
and still some unhealthy relationships.
These decisions may not been as unhealthy

as before but still unhealthy, I realize my cracks are still healing. Then I had an epiphany...this book is not just for you but it is for me also. Healing is a continuous process and as we go through this process, we must not only forgive those who hurt us but we must forgive ourselves for the hurt we endured and this is the most difficult task in the healing process. It is one thing to say something but it is an entirely different thing to do something. There is no easy route; we just have to understanding that healing is a process that may initially cause a lot of pain before true healing begins. We must find a safe zone (your Pastor, Therapist, Friend, Spouse, family, or simply someone you truly trust, if there is even a smidge of doubt, they are not the right person) and allow ourselves to be completely emotionally naked to start the cleaning process then the healing process.

CRACKED NOT BROKEN

Let me give you an example, if a patient came into my place of employment with a laceration, there are a few steps I have to take before I could prepare the wound for healing. First, I need to get an x-ray to make sure there are no residual fragments in the wound (what are you holding on to emotionally that needs to be removed?). Second, I need to soak the wound in a cleansing solution, which often causes some discomfort but allows cleaning and removing of loss debris (you have to examine your past, forgive yourself and those that hurt you by letting go of bruised emotions). After assessing that there no foreign objects lodged in the wound and it has been soaked and cleaned thoroughly, now it is time to prepare for the healing process. Finally, a numbing solution (love and support – initially this may be hard to accept but after the first couple of positive interactions loving becomes easier) is injected into the wound, the suturing process begins (emotional healing) and healing takes place. This heal process sometimes requires immobility and rest for complete healing (take time to allow yourself to heal without an intimate relationship). The part I left out pertaining to a wound analogy is sometimes if the wound began to heal improperly, it may need to be re-opened (recalling those suppressed and/or even repressed memories) prior to beginning the previously spoken process. In order for true healing to manifest, we have to identify which stage of the healing process we are in and allow ourselves time to get through each stage. We must also understand healing is a continuous process and self-love is a daily walk that we will take for the rest of our life. Now, I believe I am ready to walk with

you, side-by-side in our healing process.
Thank you for purchasing and reading this
book. I love you.